Baby Animals in the Wild!

Elephant Calves in the Wild

by Marie Brandle

Bullfrog Books

Ideas for Parents and Teachers

Bullfrog Books let children practice reading informational text at the earliest reading levels. Repetition, familiar words, and photo labels support early readers.

Before Reading
- Discuss the cover photo. What does it tell them?
- Look at the picture glossary together. Read and discuss the words.

Read the Book
- "Walk" through the book and look at the photos. Let the child ask questions. Point out the photo labels.
- Read the book to the child, or have him or her read independently.

After Reading
- Prompt the child to think more. Ask: Elephant calves learn how to use their trunks. What do they use their trunks for?

Bullfrog Books are published by Jump!
5357 Penn Avenue South
Minneapolis, MN 55419
www.jumplibrary.com

Copyright © 2023 Jump! International copyright reserved in all countries. No part of this book may be reproduced in any form without written permission from the publisher.

Library of Congress Cataloging-in-Publication Data

Names: Brandle, Marie, 1989– author.
Title: Elephant calves in the wild / by Marie Brandle.
Description: Minneapolis, MN: Jump!, Inc., [2023]
Series: Baby animals in the wild!
Includes index. | Audience: Ages 5–8
Identifiers: LCCN 2022010025 (print)
LCCN 2022010026 (ebook)
ISBN 9798885240628 (hardcover)
ISBN 9798885240635 (paperback)
ISBN 9798885240642 (ebook)
Subjects: LCSH: Elephants—Infancy—Juvenile literature.
Classification: LCC QL737.P98 B735 2023 (print)
LCC QL737.P98 (ebook)
DDC 599.6713/92—dc23/eng/20220315
LC record available at https://lccn.loc.gov/2022010025
LC ebook record available at https://lccn.loc.gov/2022010026

Editor: Eliza Leahy
Designer: Molly Ballanger

Photo Credits: Michael Potter11/Shutterstock, cover; Wirestock Creators/Shutterstock, 1; Grobler du Preez/Shutterstock, 3; Steve Adams/iStock, 4, 23tl; Sekar B/Shutterstock, 5; Shutterstock, 6; Graeme Shannon/Shutterstock, 6–7; Duncan Noakes/Dreamstime, 8; Calv6304/Dreamstime, 9, 23br; Hedrus/Shutterstock, 10–11, 23bm; YolandaVanNiekerk/iStock, 12–13, 23bl; Frank Lane Picture Agency/SuperStock, 14–15; kavram/Shutterstock, 16–17, 23tm; Eric Isselee/Shutterstock, 18 (lion); banjongseal956/Shutterstock, 18 (grass); John Michael Vosloo/Shutterstock, 19; Bkamprath/iStock, 20–21; Anton Herrington/Shutterstock, 22; Maciej Czekajewski/Shutterstock, 23tr; bucky_za/iStock, 24.

Printed in the United States of America at Corporate Graphics in North Mankato, Minnesota.

Table of Contents

Big Ears 4

Parts of an Elephant Calf 22

Picture Glossary 23

Index 24

To Learn More 24

This baby is new.
It is an elephant calf!

It stays by Mom.

It drinks Mom's milk.

It drinks three gallons
(11 liters) each day!

gallon
of milk

ear

Its ears are big.

Its skin is gray.
It has wrinkles.

wrinkle

9

trunk

The calf learns from Mom.

It learns how to use
its trunk.

The trunk sucks up water.

The calf drinks!

The trunk sprays water.
The calf takes a bath!

leaves

The trunk picks up leaves.
It brings leaves to the calf's mouth.

The calf eats!

The calf lives in a herd.

The herd lives on the savanna.

herd

Look out!

A lion hunts.

The herd stands around the calf.

The calf stays safe.
It will grow up as
part of the herd.

Parts of an Elephant Calf

What are the parts of an elephant calf? Take a look!

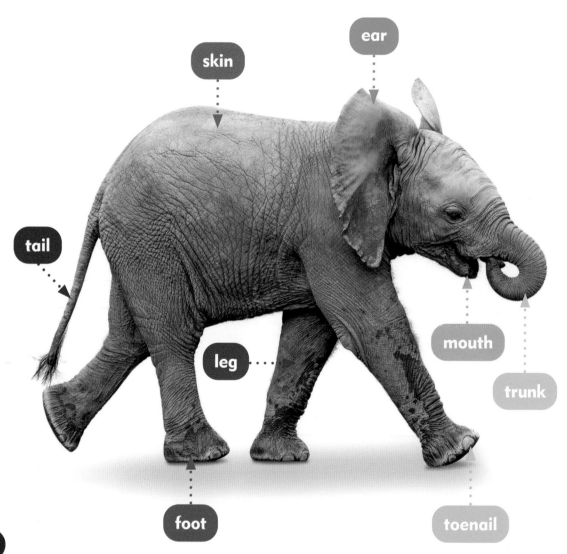

skin

ear

tail

mouth

leg

trunk

foot

toenail

Picture Glossary

calf
A young elephant.

herd
A group of animals that stays or moves together.

savanna
A flat, grassy plain with few or no trees.

sprays
Scatters liquid as drops or mist.

trunk
The long nose of an elephant.

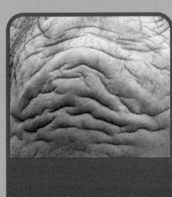

wrinkles
Lines in skin.

Index

drinks 6, 11

ears 8

eats 15

herd 16, 19, 21

lion 18

Mom 5, 6, 11

mouth 15

savanna 16

skin 9

sprays 12

trunk 11, 12, 15

water 11, 12

To Learn More

Finding more information is as easy as 1, 2, 3.

❶ Go to www.factsurfer.com

❷ Enter "elephantcalves" into the search box.

❸ Choose your book to see a list of websites.